F★A★M★O★U★S
PRESIDENTS

Photo Credits:

Pages 2-3 and 30-31—Mount Rushmore, South Dakota, is carved with the faces of four famous presidents: George Washington, Thomas Jefferson, Theodore Roosevelt, and Abraham Lincoln.

Copyright © 1999
Kidsbooks, Inc.
3535 West Peterson Ave.
Chicago, IL 60659

EYES ON AMERICA ™

F★A★M★O★U★S
PRESIDENTS

Written by
Philip Koslow

kidsbooks®
Incorporated

HAIL TO THE CHIEF

Being U.S. president is such an important job that anyone elected to it is guaranteed a place in history books. In time, some presidents fade to nothing more than a name on a list. But others use their force of personality and new ideas to make a lasting impact on America—and the world.

A NEW NATION
Nearly 170 years of British rule ended when American leaders signed the Declaration of Independence on July 4, 1776. Once the United States became an independent nation, it needed its own system of government—and a strong leader.

"WE THE ▲ PEOPLE"
Americans soon realized that they needed clear rules for who would govern the country and how. In 1787, 55 delegates from the 13 original states met in Philadelphia, Pennsylvania, to draw up a new constitution (list of basic laws and principles).

◄ SEPARATE POWERS
The U.S. Constitution was adopted in 1789. It established our three-part federal government: Congress, to make laws; the Supreme Court, to settle legal questions; and the presidency. Presidents speak for the nation, approve or reject new laws, negotiate with foreign leaders, and act as commander in chief of the military.

WHO CAN BE PRESIDENT?

The Constitution sets only three requirements for the job of United States president: A candidate must have been born in the United States, have lived here for at least 14 years, and be at least 35 years old.

THE HOME OFFICE

The White House has been the official residence of U.S. presidents and a symbol of the presidency since the early 1800s. It was known as the President's House until it was rebuilt and repainted after British troops set fire to it during the War of 1812.

MAN OF THE HOUR

George Washington, hero of the American Revolution (1775-1781), was the obvious choice to be the first U.S. president. He thought himself too old for the job (he was 56), but no one else did. He was elected unanimously in 1789.

REVOLUTIONARY HERO

In 1782, the young nation was struggling to survive, with disorganized government and low funds among its many problems. Some of General George Washington's military officers asked him to seize power and rule as king. He steadfastly refused. Many people believe that his decision saved democracy in America.

A KEY VICTORY

Washington's military skills helped win the American Revolution. One his greatest successes came on December 26, 1776, when he led a surprise attack on British forces at Trenton, New Jersey. His victory there and the Battle of Princeton eight days later helped Americans believe that independence could be won.

The ▶ winter of 1777-1778, which Washington's ragtag army spent camped at Valley Forge, Pennsylvania, was brutally snowy and cold. For the general and his men, it was a harsh test of faith in their cause. They held on and, by spring, were ready to fight again— and win.

HE COULDN'T LIE ▼

One of the most famous stories about George Washington probably never happened: six-year-old George chopping down a cherry tree, then admitting his crime, saying, "I can't tell a lie, Pa."

A CAPITAL PLAN ▲

In 1790, Washington chose the site for a new national capital. He appointed Pierre Charles L'Enfant to lay out the streets and design the government buildings. Washington never lived there, but the city's name was changed from Federal City to Washington in his honor.

MORE FREEDOM

Washington vigorously supported the Bill of Rights—10 amendments to the U.S. Constitution adopted in 1791. This historic move guaranteed U.S. citizens freedom of speech, freedom of religion, the right to a jury trial, and other important liberties.

FATHER OF HIS COUNTRY

Washington was sworn in as president on April 20, 1790, in New York City—then the nation's capital. The inauguration was held at Federal Hall, now a historic landmark in lower Manhattan. After the ceremony, cannon boomed and church bells rang.

OPEN HOUSE

President Washington and his wife, Martha, entertained three times a week at their New York residence. On Tuesdays, George hosted get-togethers for men only; on Fridays, Martha held a tea party for men and women. Thursday was the night for official dinners—and the President expected guests to be on time.

SAYING GOOD-BYE

Before he left office in 1797, Washington published a letter to the American people, urging them to put national interests above local concerns. Then he retired to his estate at Mount Vernon, Virginia, where he died in 1799 at age 67.

1st President 1789-1797

ADAMS DYNASTY

The Adams family of Massachusetts played a big part in early U.S. history. John Adams (*below*) was an American Revolution leader and second U.S. president. His son John Quincy Adams (*far right*) was the sixth president. The family tree also includes Revolution leader Samuel Adams, diplomat Charles Francis Adams, and historian Henry Adams.

TRUE ROMANCE

When he was a 26-year-old Boston lawyer, John Adams fell in love with Abigail Smith, a quick-witted beauty of 17. After three years' courtship and many passionate letters, they married in 1764.

2nd President
1797-1801

IN AND OUT OF WAR

During the Revolution, John Adams supported the war effort as a Continental Congress delegate. But he supported peace, too, by helping to write the treaty that ended the fighting. As president, he steered the U.S. away from war with France.

MOVING IN

When John Adams became president in 1797, Philadelphia was the nation's capital. By 1800, the new capital, Washington, D.C., was ready. Adams and his family were the first to live in the President's House.

TIGHT RACE

Neither John Quincy Adams nor Andrew Jackson won a majority of electoral votes in 1824, so the House of Representatives had to decide who would be president. In this cartoon, Adams (*in gray pants*) and Jackson (*in blue jacket with red sash*) "race" for members of the House.

6th President 1825-1829

FREEDOM FIGHTER ▶

In 1839, Africans aboard a slave ship rebelled. They killed the captain and cook, and demanded to be sailed back home. They ended up in Connecticut, on trial for murder. In 1841, ex-president John Quincy Adams argued their case before the Supreme Court, which ordered them freed. (The case was portrayed in the 1997 film A*mistad*.)

FIGHT TO THE FINISH

John Quincy Adams lost the 1828 presidential election, but was elected to the House of Representatives in 1830. He served 17 years there, passionately opposing slavery. In 1848, at age 80, he collapsed on the floor of the House. He died two days later.

PARTY TIME

When Washington took office, the U.S. had only one political party, the Federalists. Within a few years, it had two. The Democratic-Republican Party spoke for farmers and small tradesmen. Thomas Jefferson was the new party's first president.

AUTHOR OF FREEDOM

Jefferson believed that his greatest achievement was writing the Declaration of Independence, which helped break Britain's control over the U.S. This painting shows Jefferson reading a draft of it to Benjamin Franklin in 1776.

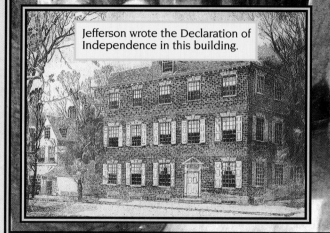

3rd President 1801-1809

◀ Jefferson, who liked to dress casually, once outraged an important visitor by greeting him in his robe and slippers.

BOOKWORM

"I cannot live without books," Jefferson once wrote. His personal library had 6,500 volumes! After his death, the government purchased the books. They became the basis for the Library of Congress, which now has more than 75 million items.

Jefferson wrote the Declaration of Independence in this building.

MAN OF MANY TALENTS

Besides being a skilled politician and diplomat, Jefferson was a musician, inventor, educator, philosopher, scientist, and architect. He designed his estate, Monticello (*left*), and buildings for the University of Virginia.

WINGS ✦ EVERY ✦ THING ✦ PROSPERS

SMART SHOPPING ▲

In 1803, Jefferson purchased France's North American territories for $15 million. That historic deal, the Louisiana Purchase, gave the U.S. control of the valuable port of New Orleans (*pictured*), and doubled the size of the U.S.

A HISTORIC FOURTH

Jefferson died on July 4, 1826: 50 years, to the day, after the Declaration of Independence was signed. John Adams—who helped draft that document, and was a political rival as well as a fellow president—died on the same day.

Jefferson ▲ appointed Meriwether Lewis and William Clark to lead a team seeking a water route from the Missouri River to the Pacific Ocean. The explorers and Sacagawea, their female Shoshone Indian guide, explored the West from 1804 to 1806.

13

CHANGING OF THE GUARD

Andrew Jackson's election in 1828 changed U.S. politics. Most of his supporters lived in the new states of the West, where all male citizens had the right to vote. (In the East, voting and politics were controlled by property owners.)

7th President 1829-1837

"TOUGH AS HICKORY"

During the War of 1812, Jackson successfully led his men through so many tough situations that they nicknamed him "Old Hickory." (Hickory trees have very hard, tough wood). The name stuck.

▼ BATTLE SCARS

At 13, Jackson joined a militia to fight the British during the American Revolution—then was captured by the enemy. When a British officer ordered young Andy to clean his boots, he refused. The angry officer struck him in the face with his sword! Jackson carried the scar as a badge of honor all his life.

THE PEOPLE'S CHOICE ▲

Unlike previous presidents, Jackson grew up poor. Everyday people saw him as one of their own. After his first inauguration, thousands of well-wishers swarmed into the White House, trampling furniture and breaking dishes. Jackson escaped out a back door and went to a hotel.

A NATIONAL HERO ▶

During the War of 1812, Jackson led a tough band of sharp-shooters that included Frenchmen, free blacks, Indians, and some pirates. On January 8, 1815, they won a smashing victory against the British at the Battle of New Orleans. The British suffered 2,036 men killed or wounded; American forces, only 21.

◀ BEATING THE BANK

Jackson's biggest battle as president was against the Bank of the United States. It was supposed to protect federal money for the good of all, but Jackson saw it as a gold mine for rich business-men. He fought to change "the many-headed monster," and won.

TRAIL OF TEARS ▶

Jackson forced thousands of Native Americans to leave their ancestral lands in the East. He ordered the Cherokee to leave Georgia. In 1838 and 1839, 4,000 of them died when they were forced to march 800 miles west—a trek known as the Trail of Tears. But Jackson could not conquer the Seminole Indians, who fought the U.S. Army in the late 1830s.

TO SAVE THE UNION

After Abraham Lincoln became president in 1861, the slaveholding states of the South seceded from the Union. Because of Lincoln's steadfast leadership in the resulting Civil War (1861-1865), most historians consider him the greatest American president.

Lincoln was born in a log cabin in Kentucky. He built this one as a young man in Illinois.

This famous photo shows Lincoln meeting with his generals during the Civil War.

A LOVE OF LEARNING

Young Abe rarely attended school—he had too much farm work to do. But he loved reading, and taught himself almost everything he knew. His love of books is reflected in this painting (based on a photo) of him with his son Tad.

16th President 1861-1865

MAKING HIS MARK

While running for U.S. Senate in 1856, Lincoln met Stephen A. Douglas in a series of historic debates. Lincoln lost that election, but his powerful attacks on slavery earned him fame. Four years later, he ran for president—and won.

▼ FOREVER FREE

In 1862, Lincoln issued the Emancipation Proclamation, declaring all slaves in Confederate states "forever free" as of January 1, 1863. "If my name ever goes down in history," he said, "it will be for this act. My whole soul is in it."

"FOUR SCORE AND SEVEN YEARS AGO . . ."

Lincoln's 1863 speech at Gettysburg, Pennsylvania, a Civil War battlefield, was only 267 words long, but the Gettysburg Address is the most famous and often-quoted speech in U.S. history.

DEADLY BLOW

On April 14, 1865, while attending a play at Ford's Theater in Washington, D.C., Lincoln was shot and killed by John Wilkes Booth. Booth did it to avenge the defeat of the South in the Civil War. He got away, but committed suicide when he was cornered in a Virginia barn two weeks later.

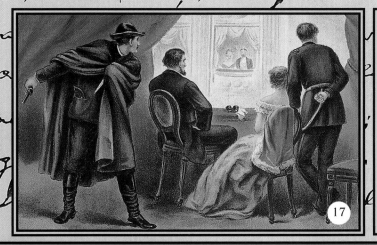

SQUARE DEALER

The late 1800s and early 1900s was a time of railroad building, manufacturing, and high finance. Theodore Roosevelt believed that the federal government should ensure a "square deal" for all Americans. As president, he curbed the power of giant corporations, settled labor disputes, set up agencies to inspect food and drugs, and protected the environment.

RUGGED INDIVIDUAL ▶

Roosevelt was a sickly child, but got strong through boxing, judo, riding, hunting, and cowpunching. In 1898, during the Spanish-American War, he commanded the Rough Riders. That regiment's famous charge up Cuba's San Juan Hill made him a national hero. (The actual charge was done on foot.)

NATURE LOVER ▼

Roosevelt doubled the number of national parks, created 51 wildlife refuges, and turned 125 million acres of public land into forest reserves.

26th President
1901-1909

"HIS ACCIDENCY"

In 1900, conservative Republicans made Roosevelt vice president to get him out of his powerful position as governor of New York. That plan backfired when President William McKinley was assassinated in 1901. "Now that cowboy is president of the United States!" exclaimed one furious political rival.

FURRY FRIEND

In 1902, Roosevelt made headlines by refusing to shoot a bear cub during a hunting trip. The following year, cuddly stuffed animals named after the President went on sale. "Teddy's bear" has been a popular toy ever since.

BULL MOOSE

In 1912, after being out of office for three years, Roosevelt ran for president again—as the candidate of the Bull Moose Party. One campaign picture showed "TR" (never shy about publicity) superimposed on a photo of a moose. Roosevelt lost that election.

BIG STICK

Roosevelt liked to quote a West African proverb: "Speak softly, but carry a big stick." To impress foreign countries with America's power, he sent a fleet of 16 U.S. battleships on a world tour in 1907-1909.

SOUTH OF THE BORDER

The Panama Canal was Roosevelt's pet project—and a symbol of U.S. power and know-how. In 1906, Roosevelt visited the site, gleefully splashing through rain and mud and taking the controls of a huge machine as he cheered on thousands of workers.

A NEW AGE

In the early years of the 20th century, more and more Americans were living in cities, and new inventions—such as automobiles, telephones, and movies—were changing their way of life. As president, Woodrow Wilson helped forge the shape of modern America.

**28th President
1913-1921**

BIG CHANGES

During Wilson's first term, he dramatically reformed the U.S. economy, making business more competitive. But he also supported measures that protected workers against being arrested for going on strike. Under his watch, Americans paid income taxes for the first time, as required by passage of the Constitution's Sixteenth Amendment.

RELUCTANT TO FIGHT ▼

When World War I broke out in Europe in 1914, Wilson vowed to keep the U.S. out of the fighting. But in 1917, after Germany stepped up submarine attacks in British waters, he asked Congress to declare war. A year later, "doughboys" (American soldiers) were fighting in France.

▲ KEEPING HOU

When White House gardeners were draft into the army during World War I, Wils arranged for a flock of sheep to live on t grounds. The woolly recruits did a fine j of keeping the grass croppe

OUT OF ACTION ▶
Wilson vigorously supported the League of Nations and other plans for world peace. His hard work won him the Nobel Peace Prize but, in 1919, he suffered a stroke. While he recovered, his wife, Edith Bolling Wilson, made many day-to-day decisions in the White House.

◀ TAKING THE LEAD ▶
After World War I ended in 1918, Wilson met with other world leaders at peace conferences in Europe. He was met by cheering crowds in Paris and London. Wilson was the first U.S. president to leave the Western Hemisphere while in office, and the first to meet with a foreign head of state.

BREAKTHROUGH
When Wilson took office, women could vote in only a handful of states—even after a voting-rights campaign nearly a century old. In 1920, the states finally approved the Nineteenth Amendment to the Constitution. It guaranteed U.S. women the right to vote.

VOTES FOR US WHEN WE ARE WOMEN

VOTES FOR US WHEN WE ARE WOMEN

FEARLESS LEADER

In 1932, U.S. voters chose Franklin D. Roosevelt (Theodore's cousin) to lead the way out of the Great Depression, which had left one fourth of U.S. workers jobless. Many went hungry, or stood in breadlines for food (*below*). Tackling the crisis, FDR declared: "The only thing we have to fear is fear itself."

CONGRESS

TO EMERGENCY LEGISLATION

◀ **NEW DEAL** ▼

During Roosevelt's first "Hundred Days" in office, 15 major laws were enacted —a record that stood until 1964. The New Deal, his economic-recovery program, reformed the banking system and put people to work building dams, parks, and highways. The WPA (*below*) was one New Deal jobs program.

Work Pays America

PROSPERITY

WORKS PROGRESS ADMINISTRATION

ON THE AIR

On March 12, 1933, FDR made his first radio broadcast from the White House to explain how he was dealing with the nation's economic problems. These popular broadcasts, which became known as "fireside chats," continued until Roosevelt's death.

32nd President 1933-1945

NEW JOB FOR A FIRST LADY

After her husband was disabled by polio, Eleanor Roosevelt began making many public appearances for him, leading meetings and giving speeches. She became well-known and admired in her own right as a tireless campaigner for human rights.

'ANDING TALL

After contracting polio at age , FDR traveled in a wheel-air and walked with the aid canes and heavy leg braces. ews photos and newsreels ways showed him from the ist up, so few Americans re aware of their dynamic esident's disability.

BREAKING THE MOLD

FDR was reelected by a landslide in 1936. In 1940, he did something that no U.S. president had ever done: He ran for a third term. Opponents condemned this break with tradition, but voters reelected FDR in 1940, and again in 1944. (He died in office during his fourth term.) In 1951, the Constitution was amended to limit presidents to two terms.

WARTIME LEADER

After Japan attacked Pearl Harbor on December 7, 1941, Roosevelt rallied Americans in a massive war effort. Between 1942 and 1945, U.S. factories turned out 300,000 planes, 87,000 warships, and 102,000 tanks, while more than 16 million men and women served in the armed forces.

THE AMERICAN CENTURY

The U.S. emerged from World War II as the most powerful nation in the world, and its citizens soon began to enjoy the highest standard of living they had ever known. Harry S. Truman and Dwight D. Eisenhower presided over this boom—and its challenges.

ON THE SPOT ▲

President Roosevelt died in April 1945, and Vice President Truman took over—as World War II was coming to an end. In July, he met with British leader Winston Churchill (*left*) and Soviet leader Joseph Stalin (*right*) to decide how post-war Europe would be controlled. That August, he ended the war by using the atom bomb, a terrifying new weapon, against Japan.

The BUCK STOPS *here!*

TOUGH TALK

Truman was known for his tough talk and impatience with slackers. "The buck stops here!" was his way of taking responsibility for the decisions he made as president. "If you can't stand the heat, get out of the kitchen" was another favorite saying of his.

Chicago Daily Tribune — Home

DEWEY DEFEATS TRUMAN

G.O.P. Sweep Indicated in State, Boyle Leads in City

◄ AN AMAZING UPSET

Political experts said that Truman had no chance for victory when he ran for reelection in 1948, against Republican Thomas E. Dewey. But Truman amazed the experts—and proved this early-edition headline wrong—by winning with plenty of votes to spare.

33rd President 1945-1953

2

◀ **HEROIC LEADER**

Dwight D. ("Ike") Eisenhower won the presidency on the popularity he earned during World War II, when he was supreme commander of the Allied forces in Europe. He planned the victorious D-Day attack of 1944, which helped turn the war in the Allies' favor.

WHO'S THE BOSS? ▲

Truman took his role as commander in chief of the armed forces seriously. When General Douglas MacArthur criticized the government's strategy during the Korean War, Truman fired him—even though Congress and the public sided with MacArthur.

▲ **UNDER THE WEATHER**

During his two terms in office, Eisenhower suffered a heart attack, a severe intestinal ailment, and a slight stroke. His health problems led to adoption of the Twenty-Fifth Amendment to the Constitution, which provides for a transfer of power in case a president is disabled.

PEACEMAKER

Eisenhower took steps to ease the tense relations that arose between the U.S. and the Soviet Union after World War II, and to end the Korean War (1950-1953).

I LIKE IKE

25

NEW IMAGE

On January 20, 1961, John F. Kennedy, 43, became the youngest man ever elected president of the United States. Although his term was cut short, he captured the imagination of Americans as few leaders have ever done.

▲ PT-109

During World War II, Kennedy skippered the PT-109, a U.S. Navy gunboat that was rammed by a Japanese warship. He earned a medal for rescuing his crew. When asked later how he became a war hero, JFK said, "It was involuntary—they sank my boat."

35th President
1961-1963

SOUNDING THE CALL

In his inaugural speech, Kennedy said, "Ask not what your country can do for you, ask what you can do for your country." He inspired thousands of young Americans to sign up for the Peace Corps, a new agency that sent volunteers to aid developing countries throughout the world.

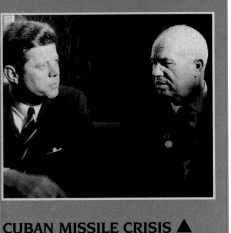

LIVING LEGENDS ▼
The dashing style and youthful good looks of JFK and his wife, Jacqueline, captivated the American public. Commentators compared the Kennedy White House to Camelot, the glittering court of Britain's legendary King Arthur.

CUBAN MISSILE CRISIS ▲
Nuclear war seemed terrifyingly possible in October 1962. Kennedy demanded that the Soviet Union remove its nuclear missiles from Cuba, just 90 miles south of Florida. After several days of tense negotiations, Soviet leader Nikita Khrushchev (*at right in a later photo*) backed down and removed the missiles.

▲ THE FINAL FRONTIER
Kennedy wanted America to explore a New Frontier: space. One of his top goals was building the U.S. space program. NASA's first big leap was John Glenn's 1962 flight—the first manned flight to orbit Earth (made in the capsule shown).

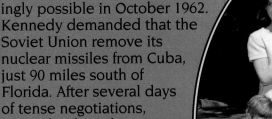

DOUBLE TRAGEDY
On November 22, 1963, John Kennedy was struck down by an assassin's bullet as he rode in a motorcade in Dallas, Texas. Five years later, his younger brother, Senator Robert F. Kennedy, was also shot to death, while campaigning for the Democratic presidential nomination.

PRESIDENTIAL SNAPSHOTS

Only a few presidents achieved greatness in office, but many made their marks on history by important achievements, mistakes, or misdeeds—or by odd twists of fate.

**17th President
1865-1869**

**9th President
Mar. 4, 1841-Apr. 4, 1841**

**11th President
1845-1849**

▲ ODD MAN O

Andrew Johnson was the f
president in U.S. history to
impeached (charged of wro
doing and tried by Congress)
1868, he was acquitted (fou
not guilty) of violating fede
laws. Years earlier, wh
Johnson was
only senator fr
the South to su
port the Uni
he narro
escaped be
hanged
enrag
Southerne

PASSING ▲ THROUGH

William Henry Harrison holds the record for shortest term in office. The 68-year-old ex-general caught a bad cold during his swearing-in ceremony, then came down with pneumonia. He died on April 4, 1841, after only a month in office.

NATION BUILDER

In 1846, James K. Polk persuaded Britain to give up the Oregon Territory. Then he started a war with Mexico that ended with Texas, California, New Mexico, and Arizona becoming part of the U.S. By the time he left office, U.S. territory had increased by 50 percent.

WING OUT ▼

Richard M. Nixon (*right photo*) was the first
. president to resign from office. He
pped down in 1975 because he
ed impeachment by Congress.
on had been accused of
ering up illegal activi-
s by White House
ployees in a
ndal called
atergate."

HEAVY HITTER ▼

At 332 pounds, William Howard Taft was the
heaviest U.S. president. (He once got stuck
in the White House bathtub!) He also was
the first president to actively campaign
for reelection, against Theodore
Roosevelt and
Woodrow Wil-
son in 1912.
(Wilson
won.)

**37th President
1969-1974**

**27th President
1909-1913**

STINY ▼

At 16, Bill
nton visited the
ite House and
to shake hands
h President John
nnedy. Clinton, who
s elected in 1992 and
6, became only the
ond U.S. president to be
eached—and acquitted.

**SUCCESS AND
FAILURE** ▶

Lyndon B.
Johnson pursued
his vision of a
"Great Society" by
pushing through
dozens of laws
that promoted
civil rights, medical
care, education,
and the creative arts.
But he is remembered
most for failing to end
the Vietnam War.

**42nd President
1993-2001**

**36th President
1963-1969**